A Fitting of Halperin's Bureaucratic Model with Domestic and Foreign Policy Events of the Vietnam War

STEVE DAFOE

A Fitting of Halperin's Bureaucratic Model with Domestic and Foreign Policy Events of the Vietnam War

PRINT BOOK ISBN 978-1-304-06308-3

Table of Contents

Part 1: Interests and Participants

Since the beginning of man's existence, organizations have been an integral part of shaping ones' beliefs and ideas about himself and that of the surrounding environment. This report deals with the individuals' ideas and how he manipulates his beliefs in others. Various examples will be shown of how the individual can shroud and misconceive his ideals for the betterment of himself, the organizations, and the country.

As pointed out by Halperin (1974:26), "All organizations seek influence" and therefore are able to pursue their other objectives and purposes. To do this requires much attention and this report deals with some of those necessities. To accomplish their wants, the organization must be effective, and this can only be realized:

> … if it's; personnel are highly motivated. They must believe that what they are doing makes a difference and promotes national interest; that the organizations' efforts are appreciate… Above all the career official must believe there is room for advancement…and that the organization is seeking to protect his opportunities for advancement. (Halperin, 1974:54).

This brings to light the importance of the participants and their interests and how these are shaped and affected by the interests of National Security, the President, and the participants respective organization.

During the postwar period, Americans have come to share various images, the majority dealing with communism either directly or indirectly, all in the name of National Security. One shared image as pointed out by Halberstam (1965:15):

> …Rarely had there been such a political consensus on foreign affairs: containment was good, Communism was dangerous, there was of course the problem of getting foreign aid bills through Congress, bills which would help us keep the Third World from Communism.

This exemplifies what Halperin (1974:22) calls ideological thinking, "characterized by a very abstract and extensive belief patter which is…characterized by emphasis on a single value, say, fighting communism…" Another shared image in the vein of ideological thinking is the American Dream. People like William Fullbright and Dean Acheson, as shown by Halberstam (1969:30), "were committed to a view of manifest U.S. destiny in the world, where America replaced the British throughout the world as the guarantor of the existing order…They believed that the great threat to the world was Communism…"

Furthermore, one very noticeable shared image is that of "American nationalism, bringing a new strong, dynamic spirit to our historic role in the world affairs…to bring it to reality elsewhere in the world…" (Halberstam, 1969:54).

It can be seen how shared images will be able to decisively shape the stand an organization or country will take on certain issues. It is a toll for perceptions of National Security. A prime example of this is in reference to Dean Acheson's hair-raising statement with regards to Communism, "…he painted a picture of a world slowly being infected by Communism, country by country, one rotten apple contaminated the barrel." (Halberstam, 1969:407). President Lyndon Johnson provides his sense of sharing this Communist image. "Added to his belief in defense spending and a need for preparedness came a very real belief in the Communist threat." (Halberstam, 1969:549).

Shared image is one technique used to get a particular stand on a National Security issue. However, as Halperin (1974:25) has suggested, "what is in fact in the national interest is often elusive despite shared images, and participants frequently find it difficult to develop a stand simply by focusing on national security directly."

Thus, participants turn to organizational interests and presidential needs to help shape their own interests. Already, it has been mentioned that organizations seek influence and therefore is constantly trying to enhance its very essence to people within the organization as well as to the outsiders. "Organizations…will see the face of an issue which affects their ability to maintain what they view as necessary capability for a variety of actions" (Halperin, 1974:27).

Each organization attempts to push for policies that will maintain its own survival. "Individuals on these staffs share…the belief that they can best judge the nation's security interests." (Halperin, 1974:27).

As Halperin (1974:39) points out, enhancement of an organization's essence is done in several ways:

> An organization favors policies which its members believe will make the organization, as they define it, more important… An organization struggles hardest for the capabilities which it views as necessary to the essence of the organization…it resists efforts to take away from it those functions viewed as part of its essence…An organization is indifferent to functions not seen as part of its essence or necessary to protect its essence…

It is plain to see the world that each organization exists in. They live every day continually convinced that their policies are in the best interests of themselves and the country. "Institutions pushing forward with their own momentum, ideas and programs which tended to justify and advance the cause of the institution at the expanse of the nation…" (Halberstam, 1969:84). Indeed, these operations were aware its people like Fullbright and Chester Bowles who vigorously objected to the "operation organized by private men who seemed responsible to no one but their organizations." (Halberstam, 1969:85).

These men exist in every organization and the essence of their operational "is the view held by them of what their missions and capabilities should be." (Halperin, 1974:28).

Assuming what has been said so far, it is inevitable that disputes over roles and missions arise inside government, particularly, the military components of the Navy, Air Force, Army, and Marine Corps. As contended by Halperin (1974:41) there are three primary areas of dispute, "(1) the struggle between the Navy and the Air Force over Naval Aviation, (2) the Army and Air Force over Combat Support and (3) the Army and the Marines over Marine participation in ground combat operations."

One example of the dispute between the navy and the Air Force is depicted by Halberstam (1969:594): "Air Force believed in air power and bombing; old-fashioned, unrelieved bombing; the Navy, anxious to show that the carrier still worked and to get its share of roles and missions in…" Much more revealing according to Halperin (1974:43) is that the "Navy sought as large a role as possible for carrier-based aircraft in an effort to demonstrate that carriers could operates as effectively, if not more effectively, than land-based aircraft. The Air Force, on the other hand, sought to restrict the role of the Navy, arguing that it could deliver weapons more effectively and more cheaply.

It has been seen what happens when organizations seek their best interests, as they perceive them to be. The disputes among participants and their interests as they pertain to their respective organizations very often lead to a lack of co-operation on the battlefield, simply because participants see their essence as primary to any other organization.

People also base the national interest in terms of presidential thinking. "Some participants…particularly in-and-outers at high levels, detect clues to the national interest in their conception of presidential interests." (Halperin, 1974:63). John Kennedy in late 1963 believed, as perceived by Halberstam, (1969:350) that his interests were pointed toward re-election, "…1964 was an election year, any delay on major decisions was healthy; if the Vietnamese could hold out a little longer, so could he…"

At the same time, however, "John Kennedy was fast learning that his personal and political interests were not necessarily the same as those of the thousands of men worked in government." (Halberstam, 1969:262).

Lyndon Johnson's interests in late 1964 were "to first help the nation (and himself) absorb the psychic shock it had just gone through…, to establish as much continuity as possible…hard decisions on Vietnam were the last thing he wanted" (Halberstam, 1969:365).

Johnson, in tradition with most presidents, depicted himself to be a man devoted to "uncommitted thinking" in his interests. An example of such thinking as staged by Halperin (1974:24) illustrates the President, "who in dealing with a particular problem will have little weight of past experience and little firsthand knowledge. Issues tend to come to him and his closes associates in an abstract or generalized form… pressure will be brought from many sides."

Therefore, presidential interests are usually the compounded views of his closest advisors. This is portrayed by Halberstam (1969:721) in reference to President Johnson.

> He was always a man who could believe in two very sharply conflicting sides of a questions and he could, right in the middle of a hard-line discussion, change and say that he, Lyndon Johnson, had the most to lose if we went to war. He would interrupt his pro-war monologue and switch sides, saying they might throw him out of office… Those people out there, he would say, don't want to go to war… And then, he was back, planning for war, talking about slipping his hand up Ho Chi Mink's leg before Ho even knew it.

Thus presidential interests can be ambiguous and vague, very much like organizational interests. The actor's personal motivation is a basic influence on his interests. (Halperin, 1974:84) explains:

For every player, any move toward action brings an element of personal challenge... involvement of his job in some degree involves himself. Attached to his position are assorted expectations in the minds of his associates... Attached are expectations of himself. Both sorts of expectations are reflected in his interests. He is man-in-office, with a record to defend and a future to advance... The personal is tightly interwoven with the institutional.

Also pictured by Halperin (1974:85) is that "a persons' position in the bureaucracy will determine what face of an issue he sees and what seems important to him." These career officials, as they are called, believe "that the government and the nation will benefit from their services at higher levels." (Halperin, 1974:85).

With this in mind, "loyalty was to immediate superior and career...", (Halberstam, 1969:344) "... those who comforted him and gave him what he was looking for had their careers accelerated."

Perhaps a typical career officer could be a stereotype of Robert McNamara who is described by Halberstam (1969:445) as having "great and forceful doubts about ... American policy in Vietnam, yet, had an equally powerful desire to stay in government, to be a player, to influence policies for the good of the country, for the ride ideas..."

Another superb analogy of a typical career officer is revealed once again by Halberstam (1969:483)

> ... the best senior boy at the old school working between the headmaster on one side and the boys on the other; or the beloved senior clerk in a great firm who anticipates every whim of his superiors and terrorizes the clerks beneath him. He was the classic civil servant, who believes he has succeeded if he meets the demands on him from the top of the matrix.

As Halperin (1974:86-87) reveals, "To be seen fighting for the organization is valued as they to get promoted." It's only natural that you jeopardize your career by making waves or going against the grain...

After all, "It was the American way, ever upward; success justified the price, longer and longer hours invested, the long day became a badge of honour, and the long day brought the greater title. Success was worth it, and after all, success in the American way was to do well." (Halberstam, 1969:639).

One old cliché is appropriate the participants in an organization, "Don't rock the boat and you won't fall out." A participant's thoughts are shaped by presidential interests, organizational demands and his expectations of himself.

Part II: Decisions

In the process of decision making, the first step is to initiate the intended issue. The main outcome will be influenced by "the standing of the participants, the rules that guide the issue through the system, the information and analysis used by participants to select from alternate positions and to argue their cases." (Halperin, 1974:99).

In seeking a decision, the motivation may "be related to particular event that creates favourable circumstances for a new decision… or ideological thinking may be the motivating factor…" (Halperin, 1974:100).

An example of the aforementioned motivation theories is presented by Halberstam, (1969:97) "he (Kennedy) turned to Reston and said that the only place in the world where there was a real challenge was in Vietnam, and now we have a problem in trying to make our power credible, and Vietnam looks like the place."

"Dramatic changes in the actions of other nations," (Halperin, 1974:101) lead participants to seek decisions. This is illustrated by (Halberstam 1969:132) an example of American hardening against Communism:

> Two events would change the American perceptions… the first event was the hardening of the Cold War… the second, the fall of China, which sent deep psychic shock waves into the American political structure. These events, coupled with the Korean War and MacCarthyism, would markedly change the American perceptions of Communism, and more important, change the disposition of high political figures to discern subtleties within the Communist World… there would be an enormous two-party consensus of anti-Communism. The only main difference was on how to implement it…

Events so unexpected as these "would have a profound effect on American domestic politics and consequently policy." (Halberstam, 1969:149).

There are "rules to the game" of introducing an issue to the system. No matter who has the "action", as Halberstam (1969:107) refers to the organization responsible for moving an issue through the government, it is essential that there is an agreement on the issue, "not only of the action bureau but also a number of bureaus within the department. In some cases, Cabinet officers will not address a memorandum unless it has also been cleared by other agencies involved." (Halperin, 1974:107).

In the book, The Best and the Brightest Halberstam, (1969:104-105) ratifies this part of Halperin's model:

> Asia was not a separate area; instead the colonies were handled through the European nations and concurrent jurisdiction was required for policy changes. That meant that on any serious question involving a territory… both the European and Asian division had to agree before the question would go to a higher authority… the French people would concur with the French policy of returning of returning to Indochina, the Asian people would oppose it… and the question would go to the nest level, where officials would bounce it back down, suggesting that everyone get together on this.

The fact that Secretary of Defense McNamara had confidence in the techniques of systems analysis and in the individual's doing systems analysis in the Pentagon, meant that they were consulted and involved in a broad range of issues." (Halperin, 1974:112). Thus, rules of the system state that personal relationships with your own department will achieve your needs or interests and consequently avoid a breaking of the rules, or more tactfully, a changing of the rules, by getting your information elsewhere." Changing the rules may involve the creation of a new channel for moving issues to decision…" (Halperin, 1974:113-114).

In the preceding paragraph McNamara had been shown to have the confidence of his subordinates as well as having confidence in them. Thus rules of the game show McNamara having total influence; "… by the rules of the game set by McNamara, he (Klattenburg) was not allowed to say what he really though, which was that the war was probably lost already, that the military's optimistic estimates were illusory…" (Halberstam, 1969:327) (A note of interest from the above quote is the military's illusive estimates proving organizational interests).

It appears as if McNamara changed the rules in gathering his information. This is an example presented by Halberstam (1969:303) "When he moved on to Vietnam, he was not aided by those bright young kids from the Defense Department… whom he usually let loose to become his own independent sources of information with which to break institutional information networks."

An example of breaking the rules is illustrated by Halberstam (1969:377) "… Schlesingers, Galbraiths, Goodwins, Kaysens … making their direct phone calls to the President, breaking regular channels with their phone calls and short cuts." This conflicts with the usual channels that Halperin's model deal with.

> The rules of the game specify what issues should move via the formal National Security Council procedures, what issues can move by virtue of a memorandum from a particular Secretary to the President, and what issues come … other special channels … there will generally be a designated standard procedure for moving a particular issue. (Halperin, 1974:107-107).

Dean Ruck, Secretary of State, was a man concerned for the rules. He is shown by Halberstam (1969:420) as "a man who believed in the processes … he said that the processes were more important than people…" Furthermore, Rusk, according to Halberstam (1969:421) "… had a great sense of the function of the office: he believed in people playing their parts, that and no more. He believed that if the Secretary and the President did not agree, it was virtually a constitutional crisis." Dean Rusk was perhaps the most ardent supporter of the rules of the game.

The decision that one is seeking on a particular issue is usually on that only the President can ratify. As Halperin (1974:116) states, "the central problem in planning is to determine how one can get the issue to the president, put him in a position where he believes he has to make a decision, and then get him to decide in one's favor."

Richard Nuestadt has said, "that perhaps the most active game in Washington is seeking to determine who has influence with the President on what issues."

To avoid destroying one's career, participants very often hesitate to push a view if they don't know who is going to be involved and who will influence the President. Participants value their relationship with the President and are "equally concerned with what their colleagues will think if their advice is rejected by the President." (Halperin, 1974:121). Thus, what happens is that a participant will opt in or opt out depending on if they want to be in the game.

An example of this opting out is shown by Halberstam (1969:216), "Rusk remained somewhat on the sidelines, caught in his ambivalence between recurring doubts about the regime and its lack of reforms…but he tended to limit his dissent." In yet another example of opting out, Dean Rusk, "…was uneasy with this kind of estimate (military) not so much because it was pessimistic…but because he was a strict chain-of-command man himself and did not like State's getting into the Defense area; in a question involving the military he had an instinct to give primacy to Defense, and not to cause problems…it was one thing for the State Department to talk about the political problems, but it was quite another for State to challenge military estimates.." (Halberstam, 1969:316).

Thus, opting out is a way of not getting into the political arena. Once a participant is involved with an issue, then it becomes a calculated game where strings are pulled to include certain participants or to exclude them by either reducing the circle or widening it. "If the president is firmly committed to moving in a particular direction, the argument can be made to him that individuals who are likely to oppose the action…should be excluded." (Halperin, 1974:125). A prime incident of this closing of the circle is revealed by Halberstam (1969:440-441):

> Vietnam gradually became a more sensitive, more delicate, and more dangerous subject. As such it became something spoken about less and less, the decisions become more and more closely held, and the principles become even more guarded with whom they spoke on the subject…Johnson limited the amount of debate, partly because debate went against his desire for consensus…The important thing was to get everyone aboard…

Halberstam (1969:492) reinforces the narrowing of the circle, "Only the very top people were involved on the decisions and the drift of it; the other, the second- and third-echelon people who had been playing some part, were moved out." One final example of narrowing the circle is quoted by Halberstam (1969:556), "Thus the decisions on Vietnam would be made by very few men, and the players would be different from those under Kennedy, … the more men who participate, the more gossip there is going to be… there would be a disagreement at the top level of government…so the way to control secrecy was to control decision making, to keep it in as few hands as possible and make sure those hands were loyal…"

Conversely, the circle may be widened to include as many participants as to make an appropriate decision. "The basic argument used for enlarging the number of participants is the doctrine that the President should hear all points of view." (Halperin, 1974:127). In this system, no participant should hesitate to view his opinion, "for the rules of the game clearly provide for his involvement should he choose to engage himself." (Halperin, 1974:128). This widening of the circle is depicted by Halberstam (1969:632) when agreement was made, "on a retaliatory strike, except Mike Mansfield, who had been invited to the meeting." This example follows Halperin's idea of expanding the circle which, "is to secure an invitation for an individual to participate in a forum…" (Halperin, 1974:128). Just as Mansfield was invited by Johnson, General Earle Wheeler was invited "to participate in the Tuesday lunch discussions at which Vietnam matters were debated", (Halperin, 1974:123), another example of widening the circle.

In order to give support to your policy, it is a well-used technique of selective information that now enters the political arena. As Halperin (1969:158-159) has theorized, to be selective means to encompass quite a few areas in the filtering out of negative responses.

Several examples of selective information appear throughout "The Best and the Brightest"; for instance, Halberstam (1969:221) writes, "Nolting would change State's reporting, and to that would not be added the military reporting, forceful, detailed and highly erroneous, representing the new commander's beliefs that his orders were to make sure things looked well on the surface." This follows in line of Morton Halperin's model of "reporting information so that senior participants will see what you want them to see and not other information." (Halperin, 1974:159). Another example of selective information involved General Paul Harkins, whose "two main distinctions during his years of service of the United States, and second, that it brought him to a point of struggle with a cast number of his field officers who tried to file realistic (hence pessimistic) reports. (Halberstam, 1969:223). Not to be neglected in this filtering out of the negative aspects is the misleading of the President, Halberstam (1969:774) states the following:

> … in the White House basement, aides culled through the reams of information coming in from Saigon and picked the items which they knew Rostow was following… They would send this up to Rostow, and he would package it and pass it on to the President….

It can be seen that the process of selective information just so that organizational interests may have an influence on the direction of foreign policy has caused great strife for Americans in Vietnam and for the public back home.

One must look at the press to see the agony that the United States suffered through. More often than not "the press influence presidential decisions." (Halperin, 1974:173). Usually, it is an excellent manner to get feedback, as a whole, from the American public.

However, the use of the press during the Vietnam was manipulation, or at least was under pressure, to report positively. Halberstam (1969:226) presents a popular and often used tool to make things look better than they actually were; "…the American Administration would have to justify a decision it had made by manipulating the facts… by trying to manage the news and events, and finally, when that failed, by constant assaults on reporters in Vietnam who continued to report pessimistically."

Staying close to Halperin's model in regard to use of the press; Halberstam (1969:701) brings out an example of a deliberate leak; "…selected correspondents from both the New York Times and the Washington Post were called in and given a deliberate leak. The judgement of the military was that it would not be a short war…but the North would not be able to withstand the American pressure that long." This deliberate leak is done for the reporters so as to establish a mutual working relationship with the White House. The reporters are "provided with leaks in return for a promise to report the information in a way that will accomplish the objectives of the President in leaking the material." (Halperin, 1974:175). Thus, a quick analysis sees that the deliberate leak in the quote mentioned is a device by the President to say that 'though the war is a little longer than we expected, it'll be over in six months'."

Eventually, the decisions are finally made, whether they have been misperceived through manipulation of the press or through the breaking of the rules of the game. The old cliché says that "actions speak louder than words." Part Three deals with how the United States acts after the President decides.

Part III: Interests and Participants

"The president tends to delay decisions and then decide as little as possible." (Halperin, 1974:235). Perhaps the "consensus for the decision depends on the Presidents vagueness." (Halperin, 1974:236). Therefore, little friction is caused if there is a decision made in vague terms. The idea is to get a broad consensus with as much harmony on the issue so that it may be implemented.

"Foreign Policy decisions made by the President must of course many times be implemented in the field by ambassadors or by military commanders." (Halperin, 1974:261). These people are no different than any other organization back in Washington, they have their own views with, of course, primary loyalty to their organization. "Subordinate officials use all the techniques in dealing with orders from their ambassador...violate the ambassador's orders...outright disobedience is not uncommon." (Halperin, 1974:262). Why?

"Believing that they are more adept at dealing with the local government...officials in the field feel that they should make policy decisions, and that Washington should simply support them." (Halperin, 1974:263). This can be seen in the following example by Halberstam (1969:261):

> The White House was beginning to see that the people who were in charge of the mission in Saigon had begun to take on the coloration of the commitment, they were more militant then Washington, more committed to Diem...

As Halperin (1974:264) points out, "Operators in the field are prone to see Washington as a great bureaucratic sludge which is either unresponsive when something is wanted or bristling with ideas that no one needs. The lack of a systematic, meaningful dialogue between Washington and the field is a severe handicap to effective coordination." This is ratified by aforementioned quote from David Halberstam.

This lack of coordination often suggested that the war was going badly but no one in Washington knew just how bad it was. This is exemplified by Halberstam (1969:341), "...the Americans in the field might not know about politics, but they knew whether or not the war was being won, and they said it was going well." Another illustration by Halberstam (1969:364):

> On November 21, Henry Cabot lodge flew to Honolulu on the first leg of a trip to Washington, where he planned to tell the president that the situation, even Lodge, who had been pushing the idea that the war was going badly, was shocked at just how discouraging it really was, and he planned to tell Kennedy that there was serious doubt as to whether government could make it...

"In many cases the ambassadors does not wish to know what is going on... the C.I.A. often operates simply without information the local ambassador." (Halperin, 1974:262). An example is depicted by Halberstam (1969:429) with regard to this, "Nguyan Khanh, ..., told his American advisors that he planned to pull a coup against the generals...word went unofficially to the embassy, which took the position that it did not want to know anything."

Indeed, communications was so deplorable that Taylor, "had gone back to Washing to clarify three problems..." (Halberstam, 1969:691).

"Field missions, like agencies in Washington prefer to act without presidential decisions" (Halperin, 1974:276). Furthermore, Halperin (1974:276) points out:

> An unwritten law in the Foreign Service is: Never ask for instructions from Washington if you can help it. It is presumed the officer in the field is familiar with official policy; in most cases he is in a better position than anyone else to decide how a given problem should be handled in the light of that policy…

This part of Halperin's theory is once again put to the test by Halberstam (1969:564), "As far as American officials in Saigon were concerned, Taylor gave them their marching orders…immediately upon his arrival. He had summoned the mission council together, that group of Americans who ran the country…and he briefed them on what he considered to be American objectives." (Halberstam, 1969:606) yet still shows but another example of American autonomy in Saigon; "While the bureaucracy in Washing was working on escalation, Taylor was negotiating the Saigon mission to virtually the same position: it would be bombing, but limited bombing." These examples clarified Morton Halperin's idea of actions without decision. To implement a vague presidential decision is up to the officer in the field who should know more about the reality of events in his environment. This further shows the lack of a co-ordinated communications system between Saigon and Washington.

In conclusion, Halperin's model does have basic criticisms. First of all, it is implemented toward America, thus raising the possibility if the model would stand up against any other countries. Second, it seems to be cross section of Halperin's own ideas and that of Allisons' model.

The model represents American politics in this regard it could be said that the model is useless to other governments. But it can also be said that there are not two governments in the world who are alike either because of geography, power, political structure, and most importantly; what motivates other governments in foreign policy. All these factors result in a differing state; Halperin's model is made to specifically for the American political system.

The model deals with the bureaucracy in a manner which identifies the stereotype image of the bureaucracy with the public. Morton Halperin reveals the most inner secrets of how, who, why, where and when things are done whether they be illegal or within the confines of the law; whether that be written or unwritten law. A very well-done model; no matter what criticisms are forwarded; to show politics in foreign policy as well as Domestic Policy; how people and governments are manipulated through organizational interests, National Security interests or Presidential interests. The model reveals how to be influential and through what formal or informal channels you tunnel your influence.

Most of Halbertsam's book could be placed to parallel the Halperin Bureaucratic Model, as has been continuously show throughout this report.

Halberstam stages examples to show the organizational interests of the military; how the President and his White House staff protect their own interests; how opting in or opting out bring various compromises within government; how the men in the field reach to decisions. Such examples, I feel, have clarified the Halperin Bureaucratic model, enough to confirm that it is a realistic viable model of how America really works.

References and Bibliography

Halberstam, D. (1969) The Best and the Brightest. Greenwich: Fawcett Publications, Inc.

Halperin, M. H. (1974) Bureaucratic Politics and Foreign Policy. Washington: The Brookings Institute.

GPT Chat-Acknowledgement of researching common knowledge definitions and terms. GPT Chat is an AI powered language model that provided insightful information in the research of this book. 2024

Quick Political Terms for the United States

1. **Democracy**: A system of government where power is vested in the people, who rule either directly or through freely elected representatives.
2. **Republic**: A form of democracy where the country is considered a "public matter" and the head of state is an elected or appointed official, not a monarch.
3. **Bipartisan**: An approach or policy that is supported by members of both major political parties.
4. **Congress**: The legislative branch of the U.S. government, consisting of the Senate and the House of Representatives.
5. **Senate**: The upper chamber of Congress, with 100 members serving six-year terms. Each state has two senators.
6. **House of Representatives**: The lower chamber of Congress, with 435 members serving two-year terms. Representation is based on population.
7. **Executive Branch**: The branch of government responsible for enforcing laws, headed by the President.
8. **Judicial Branch**: The branch of government responsible for interpreting laws, headed by the Supreme Court.
9. **Electoral College**: A group of electors from each state who formally elect the President and Vice President of the United States.
10. **Bill**: A proposal for new legislation or an amendment to existing legislation.
11. **Veto**: The President's power to reject a bill passed by Congress, which can be overridden only by a two-thirds majority in both the House and Senate.
12. **Filibuster**: A tactic used in the Senate to delay or block a vote on a bill by extending debate.
13. **Lobbying**: The act of attempting to influence legislators and government officials to enact or reject legislation.
14. **PAC (Political Action Committee)**: An organization that raises and spends money to influence elections and legislation.
15. **Primary**: An election in which voters choose candidates for the general election, or choose which candidates will represent a party.
16. **Caucus**: A meeting of members of a political party to select candidates or decide on policy.
17. **Super PAC**: A type of political action committee that can raise and spend unlimited amounts of money to influence elections, but cannot directly coordinate with candidates.

18. **Executive Order**: A directive issued by the President to manage the operations of the federal government.
19. **Impeachment**: The process by which a sitting President or other federal officials can be charged with misconduct. If convicted, they may be removed from office.
20. **Gerrymandering**: The manipulation of electoral district boundaries to favor a particular political party or group.

These terms cover a very quick spectrum of U.S. political processes and structures. Below is a more detailed list

Detailed list of US political terms

A

- **Absolute Majority**: More than half of the total number of votes or seats, including those not cast.
- **Action Committee**: A group organized to support or oppose political candidates or policies.
- **Advisory Referendum**: A non-binding vote where the results guide policymakers but do not mandate a specific action.

B

- **Bipartisanship**: Cooperation between two major political parties, typically to achieve a common goal.
- **Budget Deficit**: Occurs when expenditures exceed revenue.

C

- **Caucus**: A meeting of members of a political party or faction to make decisions or select candidates.
- **Checks and Balances**: A system where different branches of government have powers to check each other and prevent any single branch from becoming too powerful.
- **Cloture**: A procedure to end a filibuster in the Senate and bring a debate to a close.

D

- **Democratic Party**: One of the two major political parties in the U.S., typically associated with progressive and liberal policies.
- **Deregulation**: The reduction or elimination of government rules controlling business operations.
- **District**: A geographic area represented by an elected official.

E

- **Electoral College**: A body of electors established by the Constitution that formally elects the President and Vice President of the United States.

- **Electorate**: All the people eligible to vote in an election.
- **Entitlements**: Government programs that provide benefits to individuals who meet certain eligibility criteria, such as Social Security or Medicare.

F

- **Filibuster**: A tactic used in the Senate to delay or block a vote on a bill by extending debate.
- **Federalism**: A system of government where power is divided between a central authority and smaller political units, like states.

G

- **Gerrymandering**: The manipulation of electoral district boundaries to favor a particular political party or group.
- **Grassroots**: Political movements or campaigns that originate from the general public rather than from political elites.

H

- **Hard Money**: Political donations that are regulated by law and given directly to a candidate's campaign.
- **House of Representatives**: The lower chamber of Congress, with members elected based on population from each state.

I

- **Incumbent**: The current holder of a political office.
- **Independent**: A voter or candidate not affiliated with any political party.

J

- **Judicial Review**: The power of courts to declare laws or executive actions unconstitutional.
- **Justice**: A member of the Supreme Court, responsible for interpreting the Constitution and adjudicating legal disputes.

K

- **K-Street**: Refers to the lobbying and advocacy firms located on K Street in Washington, D.C.

L

- **Lobbying**: The act of attempting to influence legislators and officials to support a particular cause or policy.
- **Liberal**: A political ideology that generally supports progressive reform and government intervention in the economy and social issues.

M

- **Majority Leader**: The head of the majority party in either the House or Senate, responsible for guiding the party's legislative agenda.
- **Midterm Elections**: Elections held midway through a president's term, often affecting congressional control.

N

- **National Debt**: The total amount of money that a country's government has borrowed and owes to creditors.
- **Nominee**: A person who is selected or proposed by a party to run for political office.

O

- **Open Primary**: A primary election where voters are not required to be registered with a party to vote in that party's primary.
- **Order of Precedence**: The hierarchy of government officials and their rank or importance.

P

- **PAC (Political Action Committee)**: An organization that raises and spends money to influence elections and legislation.
- **Partisan**: Strong allegiance to a particular political party or ideology.
- **Pork Barrel**: Government spending intended to benefit specific constituents or districts.

Q

- **Quorum**: The minimum number of members needed to conduct official business in a legislative body.

R

- **Republican Party**: One of the two major political parties in the U.S., typically associated with conservative and right-leaning policies.
- **Redistricting**: The process of drawing new electoral district boundaries, usually after a census.
-

S

- **Senate**: The upper chamber of Congress, with two members from each state, regardless of population.
- **Super PAC**: A type of independent political action committee that can raise unlimited funds for political campaigns but cannot coordinate directly with candidates.

T

- **Tort Reform**: Changes to the legal system intended to reduce the ability to file lawsuits and limit damages awarded.
- **Third Party**: A political party other than the two major parties (Democratic and Republican).

U

- **Unfunded Mandates**: Regulations or policies imposed by the federal government on state or local governments without providing funding to cover the costs.
- **Unique Votes**: Votes cast by individuals who are not typical participants in the electoral process.

V

- **Veto**: The President's power to reject a bill passed by Congress.
- **Voter Turnout**: The percentage of eligible voters who participate in an election.

W

- **Whip**: A party official who helps to enforce party discipline and ensure that party members vote according to party lines.

X

- **Xenophobia**: The fear or hatred of foreigners or strangers, often influencing immigration policies and national security.

Y

- **Yellow Dog Democrat**: A term historically used to describe a Democrat who would vote for a "yellow dog" rather than a Republican.

Z

- **Zoning Laws**: Regulations that define how property in specific geographic zones can be used, impacting local development and land use.

About The Author

   The Accomplished Songwriter and Author has scored Film/Major Motion Picture and multiple TV placements including "Golden Globe, EMMY & Peoples Choice" award winning shows. Recently, "The Walking Dead" TV Series licensed 2 pieces of music for "Behind The Dead". Network & Cable TV like Sony Pictures, ABC, CTV, NBC, CBS, Showtime, MTV, BBC, Food Network, Discovery, Roku Network, Mirage Pictures and Netflix have licensed music in their lineup's.

Mirage Pictures licensed music for the movie "Sinatra in Palm Springs: "The Place He Called Home." The 'E-One Entertainment' Motion Picture, "The Big Wedding" licensed "Travelin' Jack" and starred Robert De Niro, Diane Keaton, Susan Sarandon, Amanda Seyfried & Robin Williams. The Film, "The Demented" (Producer of "Nightmare On Elm Street") licensed "Brass" in a famous elevator scene! "The Pickle Recipe", a Major Film from ABC/DISNEY licenses "End Of The Road" and star Golden Globe Nominee, David Paymer of "City Slickers" fame & Lynn Cohen from "Sex And The City" & "The Hunger Games".

A UK Major Film, "White Widow" license "Following Lincoln" and features Screen Guild Award winning actress Saffron Burrows (Boston Legal) and Kim Bodnia (Monte Carlo TV Festival Best Actor Award for "The Bridge" a Swedish/Danish Production). The French Motion Picture, "Encore Heureux" licensed "Sad Christmas" and featured a French Oscar Nomination (Globes de Cristal Awards, France) for Sandrine Kiberlain.

TV credits include from CBS & SHOWTIME "The Affair", the 2015 "Golden Globe" winner for best TV Dramatic Show and The 'LIFETIME Channel' licensing music to the "Witches Of East End" TV series. Other placements include "Children Ruin Everything at CTV & ROKU Network, the "Secret Lives of Women" at ABC TV, the "Summer Of Music" promo & "Just Tattoo Of Us" on the MTV Network , "Pit Boss" at Discovery's Animal Planet TV, "The Millionaire Matchmaker" at NBC & BRAVO TV and CMT's "Next Superstar". The AMC networks license music for the "Walking Dead" TV series which has won multiple Emmy and People's Choice Awards. The popular Russian TV Drama, "Doctor Zaitzeva Diary" license "Don't You Know" for STS Network TV.

Advertisement licensing has been accomplished with Time Warner Inc,. Red Bull Media, Marriot Hotels Chicago, Guiness Ale in Europe. Sapient Nitro and Sentry Insurance USA to name a few. The Music Lead sheets and Lyrics are published and available in E-book & Book format at Amazon, Apple Books, Kobo, Goodreads & Everand. Also available in Audiobook format at Barnes & Noble, Audible, Spotify, Amazon, Google Play, Apple and many others!

-- Red Bull Media House (UK) license 4 tunes "Storm Of Days", "You Are The One", "Finally See The Light" and "Lovin' You Ain't Hard" for TV/Film use. Music has been Licensed to Marriot Hotel and Time Inc.

-- CTV TV Network and The Roku Network license "Madrid Cafe At Sunset" in 2023-24 in the series "Children Ruin Everything"

-- "Just Like Valentine's Day" was licensed for Advertising & Corporate Video/Web usage at "GUINESS ALE" in Europe and at "The Cincinnati Children's Hospital Medical Ctr." for their corporate stakeholders.

-- AMC Cable Network/Opus1 Music license 42 songs for TV/Film opportunities. AMC boasts classic shows like "The Walking Dead", "Breaking Bad" & "Mad Men".

-- Australian TV Nine license music to "My Way" 2024.

-- A member of SOCAN, BMI and ASCAP, the music is at Spotify, TikTok, Apple, Napster, Tidal, YouTube, Google, Apple, Amazon, Deezer, Pandora, Amazon, TIDAL, iHeartRadio and here as well.

-- "Sinatra in Palm Springs: "The Place He Called Home". Mirage Pictures licensed to the movie both "Tin Pan Alley" & "Gone Baby Gone". OPUS1 Music library. 2019

-- CBS (SHOWTIME) TV Network and its new TV show, "The Affair" license "Travelin' Jack". 2015 release. The show won a "Golden Globe" for best Dramatic TV show in 2015.

-- Emmy Award & People Choice Award winner "The Walking Dead" license Music for "Behind The Dead" Season 8. 2018

-- "Encore Heureux (Still Happy), a French Major Film features "Lost Boy Lost Girl AT Christmas". 2016. Sandrine Kiberlain nominated for French Equivalent to an 'Oscar Award'.

-- ABC NEWS TV license "Never Knew You At All" for "Secret Lives Of Women". 2010

-- MTV CABLE TV license "Dancin' Shoes" for "Summer Of Music" promotion. 2010

-- "Travelin' Jack" licenced in "The Big Wedding", by Lionsgate starring Robert DeNiro, Robin Williams and Diane Keaton. 2013

-- DISCOVERY TV & ANIMAL PLANET license "Casa Loma" & "Crusin' With Grusin" for "PIT BOSS". (ongoing)

-- Major Motion Picture, "The Pickle Recipe" license "End Of The Road" in 2016. Stars Lynn Cohen (Hunger Games & Sex In The City) & David Paymer, a Golden Globe nominee from "City Slickers'.

-- MTV England "Just Tattoo Of Us" TV Program license "Best Day" for TV. 2020

-- The Food Network TV series "Girl Meets Farm" license 'Outdoor Freedom' for 2023

-- Pond 5 Music Library accepts Music 2021

-- "Anthology Of Music Lead Sheets" & "Poe-Lyrics Vol 1 and 2" are available at Amazon, Apple Books, Barnes & Noble, Kobo and other book retail sites.

-- Audible Audiobooks, Apple Books, Kobo & Barnes & Noble, Google Play, Everand have Audiobooks for distribution

AWARDS, PLACEMENTS & CONTESTS !

-- "E-One Entertainment" Major Film "The Demented" license "Brass". (Producer of "Nightmare On Elm Street") 2013.

-- NBC/UNIVERSAL TV and BRAVO license "Casa Loma","Endless Time Now" & "Crusin' With Grusin" for 5 episodes of "THE MILLIONAIRE MATCHMAKER". 2010-11

-- TIME INC. license "Wedding Morning" for partnership with GOOGLE. 2018

-- Licensed music at Sony Pictures, ABC, NBC, CBS, Showtime, CMT, Discovery TV, Direct TV, Travel Channel, LionsGate Films, Time Warner, MTV, BBC, Discovery, Netflix, Animal Planet, AMC, Seven Network (Aus) and Turner Cable.

-- CMT's "Next Superstar" licensed music for the "Meet And Greet" episodes 2011.

-- "Travelin' Jack" licensed to "Witches Of East End" Lifetime Network. (Ep 106) 2013-14

-- "Discovery Channel" and "Animal Planet" License "Never Knew You At All" for episode "UnderDog". 2012

-- "GUINESS ALE" (Ireland/Europe) license "Just Like Valentine's Day" for Advertising & Corporate Video for their World Distribution Partners 2012

-- SapientNitro license "Finally See The Lite" for Major TV Advertising. 2013

-- Hey Advertising, Seattle , Washington license "Finally See The Light" for Audio Synch & Advertising opportunities. 2015-16

-- OFF BROADWAY THEATER New York City (Space 122) license "Every Street" & "Carter's Revenge" in "MONSTER". SOLONOVA Arts Festival 2010

-- UK (United Kingdom) Songwriting contest . "Won't Be Hurt Again", (Finalist in Acoustic) 2011.

-- TIME WARNER & TRU TV license "Casa Loma" & "Crusin With Grusin" for "IT ONLY HURTS WHEN I LAUGH" 2010-11

-- "Doctors Zaitzeva Diary" license "Don't You Know" for STS Russian Network TV. Made-For-TV Serial Production. 2012

-- "CIVIL WAR" DVD license "Racing Back Through Time" and "All Alone". Kestner Prod. North Carolina.USA

-- "Serpo" licensed by Optique Salon Mgt. Software.(Advertised in Canadian Salon Magazine) 2011 (www.optiquesms.ca)

-- Music is licensed to SUBWAY RESTAURANTS - Subway is the world's largest restaurant chain. 2016

-- Music licensed to PLAYNETWORK, DMX, AQUASOFT, CLEAR CHANNEL and KIRUSA, all major CMS providers.

-- "If You Have The Time" licensed by Salsa Creative Inc (Ad Agency) in Dover, NH for TV Media.

-- "VIETNAM WAR" DVD license selected music.(US future release) Kestner Productions. North Carolina.USA

-- 2008 MTV-VH1 "SONG OF THE YEAR" (October) "You Are The One" placed #2 in "FOLK" Category. "ACOUSTIC SONG OF THE MONTH" for "BLACK GHOST" (Roots/Acoustic) at BROADJAM.COM 2008

-- Rosenklang/AudioSparx Music license 450 + Songs in Multi Genres for Digital & Streaming & CD release at I-Tunes, Spotify, Amazon , Google, YouTube, etc..

-- WINNER Of PEER REVIEW (over 100,000 members)in the "LOVE JOY CONTEST" at BROADJAM.Com 2006

-- 2004 MTV-VH1 "SONG OF THE YEAR" Contest...#4 placement for "DESERT SUN" in "FOLK" Category.

-- 2010 -2015 EOS Music (a partner of SIRIUS Radio) pick up 60+ songs for Web Channel play to Corporate clients.

-- 2010-Current. Over 440 songs for Ringtones placed with Verizon, Sprint, Muzak, Canadian/US Telecos and Boost Mobile Wordwide.

-- Nominated for Cultural Heritage Award in TV and Media in Thunder Bay. 2010

-- TU BETA TS'ENA (Water Is Life) a Canadian Film license "Matthew's Song" 2009

-- UK (United Kingdom)Songwriting contest 2010. "Love And Leaving" a Semi-Finalist in Adult Contemporary Category. 2010

-- Walleye Magazine--Story Dec 2014, Thunder Bay, Ontario. http://www.thewalleye.ca/december-2014/

-- "CINCINNATI CHILDREN'S HOSPITAL MEDICAL CENTER" license "Just Like Valentine's Day" for Corporate and Web Video. 2012

-- GAME SHOW NETWORK TV/ SONY Pictures license music (Casa Loma) for "HIDDEN AGENDA" (1 episode) 2010

-- "If I Asked" licensed the "CW TV" Network. (Pitched by Canvas Publishing) 2019

-- Bravo TV license "Birthday Rock in NY' for "Ink Masters TV". 2020

-- GIANTS TV/Slideshow uses "Shaun Conway's Song" for background. Shown on SHAW Cable TV. 2020

-- Netflix, Apple TV & Crave TV have music licensed.

-- CBC GEM 12 minute short film (TABANCA) license "Never Leave Us Behind" KAROKE scene for 2 minutes. Dampened by office life during a wet Vancouver winter, a genderqueer Trinidadian woman, Marlinn, misses out on the chance to celebrate Carnival season back home. Until, one night, they discover that the power of masquerade is within them no matter where they are. 2023

PUBLISHING & CD COMPILATIONS!

-- USA Property & Car Casualty Insurer, Sentry Insurance License "Travelin' Jack" for National TV Ad. 2013

-- Travel Channel "Bizzare Foods America" license "Truck Driver Joe". 2015

-- Wenner Media, New York license "Tin Pan Alley" & "Travelin' Jack" for Audio Sync work. They own "Rolling Stone Magazine"& "US Weekly". 2016

-- MAX.Films (Germany) License "Jack Travels' for Advertising in Germany. (2014)

-- Mobile game Vulkan Club in Russia license "American Holiday Jazz" for Mobile & Internet Applications. 2015

-- Crucial Music. Winter 2021-22. Crucial has 6 pieces that have been placed in 4 TV shows and 2 Major Motion Pictures.

-- AMC Network and Sister networks IFC and the Sundance Channel License 40 songs. Produce TV programs such as "Mad Men," "Breaking Bad" & "Walking Dead".

-- Animal Planet TV Network license music in "Pitbulls And Parolees" since 2009-13 seasons.

-- Red Bull Media House in Great Britain Sync license 4 Folk/Alt. Country tunes "Storm Of Days", "You Are The One", "Finally See The Light" and "Lovin' You Ain't Hard" 2012 (Getty/Pump Audio)

-- #1 Song Of The Month (Alt Country) "If I Asked" Jan 2013.
OUR STAGE (MTV Affiliated).

-- "A COLLECTION OF SONG POEMS" (PoeLyrics)(100+ Titles). Published by LULU BOOK Publishing. 2011

-- 2009 "Holiday Wish" compiled onto "HOLIDAY ALBUM 2009" for limited Release in the United States.

-- MUSIC PUBLISHING--(current or past) SMASHTRAX Publishing,(BMI), (Los Angeles), NBT Records (West Virginia), AUDIOSPARX (Florida), MERNEE Records (Alabama) and MUSIC ET ALL Publishing,(BMI),(Los Angeles).

---- #1 Song Of The Month (POP)"Question Of Love" May 2017 @ OUR STAGE (MTV Affiliated)

-- Map Communications Ltd.(400 employees), a Industry leading Specialized Call Ctr. in Chesapeake Virginia license 30 Songs for their business 'Phone On-Hold' needs. 2011

-- "ANTHOLOGY OF MUSIC LEAD SHEETS" (2003-2006.) Published by LULU Book Publishing. 2011

-- "Kitchen Pie" licensed to "Food Paradise" on the TRAVEL CHANNEL. 2014

-- 2006 "Black Ghost" pressed on "RIDE THE TRAIN" Vol # 32. Distributed Worldwide by NBT Records. West Virginia. USA

-- Independent Living Partnership Company License "Nonie's Song" for the Short Film "First 20 Years" for Corporate use. 2012

-- SOUNDEXCHANGE reports Radio Airplay on KJAZZ (United Kingdom). Live365, JANGO Air, KNFA Radio, Canada Air FM, RUFUS Radio, Muzak Radio and PlayNetwork Radio. 2011

-- #1 Song Of The Month (ACOUSTIC) "Love And The Leaving" Feb 2012. OUR STAGE (MTV Affiliated)

-- Bayview Magazine--Premier Publication in North West Ontario does a feature story. Spring 2013.

-- Animal Planet TV network and "Underdog To Wonderdog" licence music. 2010

-- NEW YORK UNIVERSITY license "Travellin' Jack" & "And Can You" in "THE JOURNAL" (Trailor) 2012.

-- MARRIOT INT'L HOTEL in Chicago, USA License "LaSalle Street" for Corporate Website usage.

-- "HOME FOR THE HOLIDAYS" licensed by NY Greetings Communication, Slovenia. TV Commercial 2016

-- CW TV Network & HN Media License "If I Asked" For Nwired & MeTV. 2019

-- MTV, OXYGEN TV Networks license "LASALLE ST." & "TRAIN TRACK GUITAR" for TV/Film.

-- TINDERBOX Music Library cleared and Licensed "Dance Pop One" to Shows:
"Take"- E!TV Network/Comcast
"Bad Girls Club" - OXYGEN Network
"Keeping Up With the Kardashians" - E!TV Network/Comcast
"Road Rules - The Real World" - MTV Network (All Shows)
"Total Divas" - E!TV Network
"The Real World" - MTV
"Best Ink" - OXYGEN Network

"The Ruckers" - WE Television--

-- "Dusty Roads" is in Australian Media released for Radio Airplay 2018

-- Israeli Short Film (Eti Tritto) ..."Casus Belli" license "Lasalle St" and "Bright Lites City Nights". 2008
https://www.youtube.com/watch?v=PctOsuyrmKI

-- "Best Of Top Gear" TV (BBC) license Music current season. 2.54 million viewers make it BBC top 2
program. 2020

-- Danish TV and the TR KKERDRENGENE 2 (Trekker Boys) license music 2024-25

-- "On Any Given Nite In LA" licensed to "Women Of Substance Radio. 2021

MORE LICENSING & CHARTS

-- Motion Picture (UK) "White Widow" license "FOLLOWING LINCOLN". Stars Kim Bodina, an
Award Winning actor (Monte Carlo Film/TV) from "The Bridge". Saffron Burrows won the "Screen
Actors Guild Award" for "Boston Legal".

-- DISCOVERY HEALTH TV license "Appalachian", "Casa Loma" & "Crusin' With Grusin" for "BABY
MADNESS AND CANDID KIDS" 2009.

-- Australian cooking game show "My Kitchen Rules" license "Gone Baby Gone". 2017

-- Travel Channel and "Food Paradise' license "Kitchen Pie". 2014.

-- 'Travelin' Jack' licensed (Via Getty Images) to Hanson Media house (Washington, USA) for The
Spectator Hotel.(Named #1 City Hotel Continental U.S. 2016

-- ROYALTY NETWORK & Perpetual Music Group License "Travelin' Jack" & "Orchestral Scape 1".
2017-18

-- MTV Cable TV Networks license "Travelin' Jack" and "Love And The Leaving" for TV/Film. 2011

-- Pump Audio License 'Tin Pan Alley' to "Studio Tuumant Ol" for Web Advertising in FRANCE. 2017

-- External Distributors of music are: Amazon MP3, Google Music Store, Nilsson Online Distribution,
Spotify, MySpace Music, YouTube Music, Rumblefish, Verizon, Apple I-Tunes, I-Tunes (Worldwide),
Ruckus, Beats Music, Simfy, Groove, LAst.FM, USA Digital Distributor #1 (US, Canada telcos),
International Distributor (EMEA, LATAM).

-- "Dance Pop One" licensed for NASCAR and Sports Promos by Major Cable TV network. 2017

-- WEDDING MORNING (JAZZ INSTRUMENTAL) licensed for Conference Promo Video by TEXAS
4-H YOUTH DEVELOPMENT. 2016

--Scientia Software License "RailRoad Steel Guitar" & "Guitar Americana 13" for Mobile Applications.
2015

-- Wenner Media Online license 'Tin Pan Alley' & "Travelin' Jack' for New York Advertising House Multi-Media Needs. 2016

-- AlmoTech Digital Music license "Just Like Valentine's Day" background for Web Marketing, Retail, Hotels Usage. The UK & France. 2016

-- The FARM Channel license "Tuscan Vinyard Walk" for DVD/Video promo. 2016

-- S&P TOP 100 CORPORATION license "LASALLE ST." for Convention/Video/Web usage. 2009

-- Documentary "Arizona Storm' license "Stormy Swamp Guitar" (includes web-only videos, webcasts, podcasts, web site audio) L. Coleman Photography. 2017

-- "Music for the Suicide.TV suicide prevention project" 'You Are The One' licensed here. 2010. Video at https://vimeo.com/73416599

-- "Just Like Valentine's Day" licensed for DVD , Web Podcast and Internet Broadcast for Malibu Media. 2017

-- Performing Rights Organizations (PRO) such as ASCAP has 482 registered songs, BMI has 117 and SOCAN has 1,011 songs & 88 TV/Movie titles registered.

-- Blue TV (Netherlands) license "End Of The Road" for TV show "Bonnie & Clide". 2009

-- Tinderbox Music license 'Travellin' Jack' for use at MTV productions, VH1,The Discovery Channel & National Geographic. 2017

-- Int'l Radio Licensing of 50 + songs for Romania Audio & Radio 2017. (1 million plays+)

-- OPUS 1 PROD.MUSIC LIBRARY license 3 pieces for BBC TV/Film. 2018.

-- TONO is the Norwegian collection society/PRO-- Network TV (Norway) license 3 songs. 2020

-- Fiji & New Zealand TV license Music. 2019

-- "China T151" Train Network & Transportation System license music. 2019

-- MTV CABLE TV Networks license "Carter's Revenge" & "Love And The Leaving" for TV usage. 2017

-- Hearst Esp aa S.L License 'Jazz At Night'. Spain's Biggest publisher. 2020

-- 250 songs have been #1 at MP3.COM, Radio Indy, Indie Music, Number 1 Music/My Space & MyRecordLabel, Audiostreet, Our Stage, Reverb Nation, A&R Select & I-Like!

-- Animal Planet Network License "Guitar Pick" for Various TV shows. 2021

-- Norske Rednecks TV. 2020. Norwegian TV license "Twang That Guitar"

-- TIDENS TEGN TV (Denmark) 2020. License "Classy Peppy Lounge"

-- Music licensed to Discovery Health Network/ Bravo/ GSN & TruTV. Shows include "Hidden Agenda" & "Only Hurts When I Laugh". 2010-19.

-- MINIONS TV (Singapore) (2015) license Music. "Travelin' Jack"

-- Shutterstock Music partners with POND5 artists 2022

-- "Travelin' Jack" has 2 million plus radio plays in 3 months in Brazil and Mexico. 2023

-- BIZZARE FOODS--(PITTSBURG ON "THE TRAVEL CHANNEL") -- Travel Network 2011 license music

-- "Molly's Love" licensed to the Rensselaer Polytechnic Institute for Advertiement. It is a private research university in Troy, New York, with an additional campus in Hartford, Connecticut.

-- "Song For Baylee Almon" licensed to Japanese Media for Internet Advertising. 2024

www.ingramcontent.com/pod-product-compliance
Lightning Source LLC
Chambersburg PA
CBHW080352290526
45791CB00009BA/2850